eart of a Woman   Singin'   s

the Pulse of Morning   Sha   ?   All God's Children

A Brave and Startling Truth   Life Doesn't Frighten Me   Phenomenal

iie   Oh Pray My Wings Are Gonna Fit Me Well   Weekend Glory   Our

y Like Christmas   Wouldn't Take Nothing for My Journey Now   I Shall

g?   All God's Children Need Traveling Shoes   My Painted House, My

ghten Me   Phenomenal Woman   And Still I Rise   Just Give Me a Cool

ell   Weekend Glory   Our Grandmothers   I Know Why the Caged Bird

d Swingin' and Gettin' Merry Like Christmas   Wouldn't Take Nothing

haker, Why Don't You Sing?   All God's Children Need Traveling Shoes

Truth   Life Doesn't Frighten Me   Phenomenal Woman   And Still I Rise

re Gonna Fit Me Well   Weekend Glory   Our Grandmothers   I Know

of a Woman   Singin' and Swingin' and Gettin' Merry Like Christmas

Maya Angelou

The Poetry of Living

Maya Angelou
The Poetry of Living

Margaret Courtney-Clarke

Foreword by Oprah Winfrey

DESIGN BY ERIC BAKER

CLARKSON POTTER / PUBLISHERS / NEW YORK

Grateful acknowledgment is made to Random House, Inc., for permission to reprint excerpts from: *Even the Stars Look Lonesome* by Maya Angelou. Copyright © 1997 by Maya Angelou. "Our Grandmothers" from *I Shall Not be Moved* by Maya Angelou. Copyright © 1990 by Maya Angelou. Reprinted by permission of Random House, Inc.

Published by Clarkson Potter/Publishers, 201 East 50th Street, New York, NY 10022. Member of the Crown Publishing Group.

Random House, Inc. New York, Toronto, London, Sydney, Auckland
www.randomhouse.com

CLARKSON N. POTTER, POTTER, and colophon are registered trademarks of Random House, Inc.

Printed in Japan

Library of Congress Cataloging-in-Publication Data

Courtney-Clarke, Margaret, 1949-
Maya Angelou: the poetry of living/Margaret Courtney-Clarke; foreword by Oprah Winfrey.
I. Angelou, Maya. Pictorial works. 2. Women authors, American—20th century Biography.
3. Women civil rights workers—United States Biography. 4. Afro-American women authors Biography.
5. Angelou, Maya—Appreciation. I. Title.
PS3551.N464 Z55 2000
818'.5409—dc21
[B]   99-34225

ISBN 0-609-60458-9

10 9 8 7 6 5 4 3 2 1

To Caylin Nicole Johnson

Contents

Foreword

BY OPRAH WINFREY

The first time I read Maya Angelou's *I Know Why the Caged Bird Sings,* I thought I was being introduced to parts of myself.

> *What you lookin' at me for*
> *Didn't come to stay*
> *Only come to say*
> *Happy Easter Day*

This passage from the text of the first page of her autobiographical journey was a sense memory, a note from the formative pages of my own life.

I'd memorized that same poem and recited it on a stage in Mississippi much like the stage in Maya's hometown of Stamps, Arkansas. I too was raised by a strict Southern mother of the church—head of the usher board, no-nonsense grandmother.

I was raped at nine and felt as lost and as desolate and guilty as Maya did at seven.

I knew this girl, Marguerite Johnson. I was this girl. For the first time in all my reading years (I'd been reading Bible stories since the age of three), there was finally a story about me. Someone who felt like me. Saw the world through my eyes. Knew me. I felt validated. I felt I had a chance in the world to do something and have a life of my own choosing. I felt not defined by my past, my misplacement—separations from my family, abuse, trouble, pain—I felt strengthened by it. I read *Caged Bird* again and again throughout high school. It became my talisman. Maya Angelou, my Shepherd. My hero.

Years later, when she was on a book tour, I felt privileged to be able to share a private moment with her. I was doing a show in Baltimore called *People Are Talking.* I had a cohost, but I knew an interview with Maya Angelou with two people, one of whom was not familiar with her work, would do neither her nor the program any justice. Besides, I wanted this one badly for myself.

I was afraid she'd say no—but mustered the courage to ask for a five-minute interview. I promised to be at her hotel to set up and not take more than five minutes of her time. She said yes. And though I could have talked for hours, I stopped in five minutes as

promised. At which point she said—
"Mmmm, who are you, girl?"

It is a friend-kinship that runs deep and wide. To have a heroine come off the page of a book that by its own right had given me hope and insight and a better way of being with myself and which had become a part of my life was nothing less than a miracle—a fantasy I could not have ever imagined. Though I met Maya in mid-adulthood, I feel as though I have known her all my life. I have grown so much with her—how did I manage to grow up without her? She has been a constant source of wisdom, enlightenment, and joy.

Not long after our first interview, I was invited to her home for a "real visit." She cooked my favorite meal, smothered chicken with rice, and we read poetry out loud while lying on the floor in our pajamas.

I thought: I have nothing else to live for, no more dreams. I am in Maya Angelou's home. I have read all of her books. I know many of her poems by and through my heart. She has been a source of strength and courage through the spoken word to me when I knew no other, and now I've lived to experience the day she's reading out loud to me. There have been many hours since that I've treasured with this woman whom I now call my mother-sister-friend, but that first visit was what I call a full circle HIGH C— hold the note a moment! I felt like I'd finally found home.

It was just the beginning. The journey to know myself—to understand life, to laugh and to completely love her—has been made richer, and has been deeply enhanced because of Maya.

She has been my counsel, consultant, advisor, shoulder to cry on, Rock, Shield, Protector, Defender, Mama Bear, and Mother-Sister-Friend.

I have spent hours at her kitchen table eating homemade biscuits and gravy from last night's dinner, laughing about meaningful and often mindless matters until the tears were rolling and so were we, falling out of our chairs, slapping our knees, heads thrown back, in raucous howls of glee.

And at other times, while sitting at the same table or on the same table or on the side of her four-poster brass bed, receiving quiet counsel. Always listening—listening, trying to take it all in. The root of her: Her wisdom. Her Clarity. Her Courage. Her willingness to keep standing. Her abiding faith. Her largesse. Her certain way of being in this world. Her confidence—that she is indeed God's child—sent here on earth for a little while to do His bidding.

She is intolerant of self-imposed ignorance, chaos, confusion, foolishness. She is a true Poet. She doesn't waste words. She uses them wisely and so well that always when I'm around her, I feel as though my mind and spirit are expanding.

I often take notes. Some of my best lessons and enlightened moments have come from her. My favorites:

◆ When people show you who they are—believe them. The first time.

◆ Why do you have to be shown twenty-nine times *before you see the truth?*

◆ Courage is the most important of the virtues—without it you can't practice any of the others consistently.

◆ In God you move and breathe and have your being. God wants your service. Show him what you can do.

◆ Why are you always so concerned about other people's criticism of you—those people can't hold a candle to the light God already has shining on you.

◆ In the Eye of the Storm, in the Heat of the Flame, say Thank You—for your faith that deliverance is coming.

She is a constant force of inspiration. I know she's always ready for whatever is needed. Her great gift to all who love her is that each of us feels most loved by her.

I had a grand week-long party to honor her seventieth birthday on a cruise ship to the Mayan ruins. Two hundred of her dearest friends were aboard and all felt that they were the special chosen friend for the celebration. And indeed each one of us had been chosen.

I consider it God's gift to me—a Blessing Incarnate—to witness and experience Maya's grand open heart. Her willingness to serve.

Introduction

"Only equals make friends,
every other relationship is contrived
and off balance." — **MAYA ANGELOU**

It was early 1987, and I found myself with my camera in Northeastern Nigeria, near Lake Chad in a village whose name I have chosen to forget. I was traveling alone. Red sand blew in with the dry West African wind—the one they call the *Harmattan*—and had closed roads and airports. My room was essential: bed, table, chair. There was no electricity. The sole small window had no glass pane. By night, mosquitoes feasted on me. Malaria and dysentery were playing havoc with my body, and self-pity was controlling my mind. By day I sat on the side of the road waiting for a vehicle, a truck, mule-cart, camel, whatever, to transport me and my cameras somewhere—anywhere—else. But I had one consolation. With my few personal belongings I had carried with me five paperback books: the autobiographical writings of a woman named Maya Angelou. These paperbacks were torn, yellowing, grubby, for this was not their first trip with me. I considered them part and parcel of my survival baggage.

When I needed it most these writings would offer me courage first of all, and then wisdom and humor, strength and dreams, passion and endurance, poetry and ideas. As I noted in my journal on February 4, Angelou's *Singin' and Swingin' and Gettin' Merry Like Christmas* took the gloom out of my day, in parts so hilariously funny I even laughed. Her books were the ideal companion (and consolation), for they told me that someone else had survived the pain, loneliness, and the hardships of being in a "foreign" land and a single woman on the African continent. I drew strength from Maya's autobiographies. Spiritual strength, because she believed wholeheartedly in herself, knew where she had come from and where she was going. Physical strength, because she is strong and fearless. This struck me all the more forcefully because there are critical differences between us. Maya is American. She is also an African American. I am African born, and I am a white woman, raised in Namibia under the unspeakable apartheid. Although I had long since left my country of birth to settle in Europe, at heart I remained an African. I remained forever fascinated by—and tolerant of—the splendor and hostility of Africa, her wealth and poverty, her thrilling variety of peoples and cultures, her complex history. Later, through the magnificent art of Africa's women, I came to meet Maya Angelou. While I was taking photographs for the book on West Africa, it happened that someone sent Maya a Christmas gift of my earlier book, *Ndebele: The Art of an African Tribe*. Evidently it piqued her curiosity, since she sent me an invitation to visit her at her home in Winston-Salem, North Carolina. I was honored, of course, but I was also somewhat intimidated. But as I and so many others of her "extended family" have discovered, she has an extraordinary gift of making others feel comfortable and at ease. It was to be the first of many visits.

She listens to you: she hears you. And she answers with just the right words, words that are, as one person I interviewed for this book said, "spun gold." What Maya and I have in common is that neither of us is what we seem, and this partly explains our mutual attraction. I appear to be a European but in fact I was born and bred in Africa, with an innate understanding of Africa; I have dedicated most of my life to documenting Africa's people and art. Maya, a black woman, appears to be an African, but in fact is American, born and bred in the United States. And yet our differences did not divide us: they brought us together, in a meeting of minds, which has been for both of us, perhaps, a cross-fertilization of African-Americanness. As she says, "I am who I am because you are who you are." Since then Maya and I have continued to share countless moments of spun gold speaking together about Africa. We have pored over thousands of photographs I had taken of people and places in Africa, which she feels are her people, her places. Eventually we collaborated on two children's books, and she wrote the foreword to my book, *African Canvas*. As a result I spent hours, and then days, which turned into weeks with Maya in her home, in her kitchen, in her garden, in her office. I followed her around America and then the United Kingdom on seminars and lectures. I attended inaugurations of centers for abused children and children's libraries. We autographed each other's books at stores and conventions.

And still I had never photographed her. For me—as a photographer—this proved to be a major lesson in self-control, but also in choosing priorities. For one thing, I had learned in Africa that if I wanted to win people's trust, a whole string of priorities came before the quick and easy option of firing away with my camera. For years I observed Maya's movements—slow movements, while she was chopping onions, dissecting a chicken, elegantly prancing and dancing across the kitchen floor wearing a wide-brimmed hat and concocting a marinade for half an ox to be barbecued for some special occasion. I listened endlessly to fascinating conversation as she shared her ideas with family, friends, and acquaintances. Often her captivating voice would slip into poetry or, as she herself calls it, *poesia*, then into prose. And if the Ashford-Simpsons were visiting, words would miraculously transform into music, and the music into life, and the party would begin. I missed many an "opportuni-

ty" to capture these moments. Eleven years later the memory of so many visual jewels culminated in the idea for this book.

"The book has got to be about life," said Maya on approving this project. "Otherwise it's not about me." In any case she has already told about her own life in her autobiographies, and more eloquently and honestly than anyone else could. This book then is about life recounted by those whose lives have been touched and even changed because of Maya. She has touched the lives of all of these people and inspired them through her convictions on unconditional love, family loyalty, education, faith, compassion, dignity, laughter, hard work, patience, sharing, confidence, healing, truth, forgiveness. Their lives, their words, their insight may touch your life, too. To me Maya is pure inspiration, a beacon. Maya compares life to a big umbrella with a lot of people—her extended family, as she calls us—standing under it. "Trust me," she says, "I'll trust you (and dare to pry myself loose from my ignorance)."

Through her I have learned about humor. She teaches us that from the most uncompromising negative, from desperate circumstances, it is possible to come out of it with the ability to smile on life. If you ever meet her, whatever the subject matter of the discussion, she will produce an infectious moment that not only reveals that wonderful smile of hers, those teeth, but which has everybody else laughing with her.

— JON SNOW

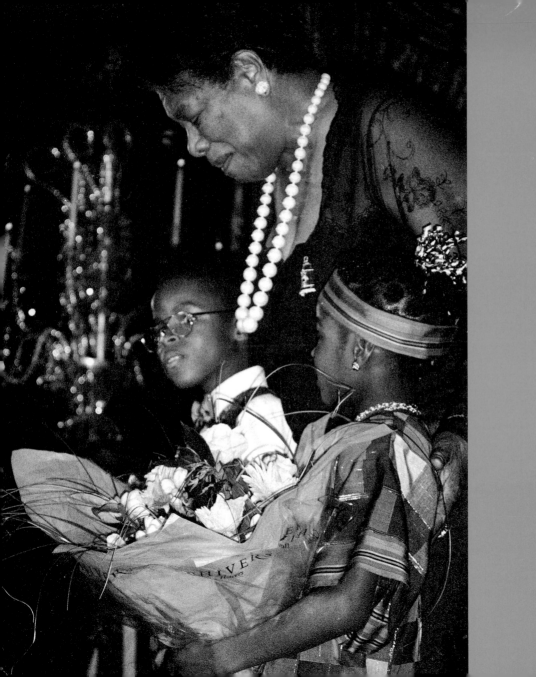

Maya's message to young children is: Laugh as much as you can! Take every opportunity to rejoice. Find the humor in life at every opportunity. Find the opportunity to rejoice. "A cheerful spirit is good medicine and sometimes a good laugh can be as healing as an aspirin!"

— DEFOY GLENN

Maya brings people together from such diverse backgrounds—throws everyone into a giant melting pot—one makes the most incredible friends that way. In Maya's words, "Folks reach out to folks," exchange ideas.

— CAROLE LEAHY

She takes time. She looks you in
the eye. There is nothing cursory ever about
the way she deals with you because what is
important to her is your personhood, your
womanhood, your manhood, your essence of
potential as a child. So for her each of us is an
opportunity to place another star in the
constellation of life.

—— AMELIA PARKER

Maya has the capacity to make one feel a part of a family. She is genuinely interested in you—for no other reason than what she is. Then you become an affirmation of her. When I had just taken the Chairmanship at Howard [University], Maya came by, as a friend, and talked to the students. She put her hand on me and said, "This is my sister; we are giving you our best."

— ELEANOR TRAYLOR

"When you learn, teach.

When you get, give."

— MAYA ANGELOU

If you have an issue, a problem that you don't understand, Maya reflects it for you very carefully, both through her words and the way she lives. More than a role model she is a reflection, a reflection of who I can be and how to find my own growth and how I can develop.

— JANICE JONES

She recognizes the divinity in everyone. The way she talks to people, the love that she extends to them, it bounces right back to her. You cannot give what you don't have. Maya has this reservoir of love for people and that's why they love her, because it's like a mirror image.

— LOUISE MERIWETHER

Maya's intense focus is impressive. Many people who meet life with such enthusiasm skip from one topic or project to another, completing none. Maya focuses on the topic or task or person in front of her, perfecting her contribution and making you feel important by bringing serious consideration to the problem you brought her, or by expressing happiness and encouragement over any achievement you shared with her. When she feels your behavior or attitude can stand improvement, she is very serious and, squirm though you might, you can't get away, and you know she is right and is making an investment in your growth.

— ALICE WINDOM

Maya just gives you everything!

— VALERIE SIMPSON

Maya takes the high road and moves ahead in life. And that is very instructive to people around her—never withholding anything, always being forthright.

— RUTH B. LOVE

Maya Angelou entered our lives at Virago in 1984, when we first published *I Know Why the Caged Bird Sings*. "Entered our lives" is too tame. She danced, sang, and laughed her way straight into our hearts. She brought us a best-seller, but more than that, she brought us a reminder that the human need for dignity and recognition is a gift easily given to one another, but also frighteningly easy to withhold.

— LENNIE GOODINGS

Maya has long arms. Big arms. When I close my eyes and think of her, I think first of her arms. Her smile and her arms. And I'd say it's the arms because I met Maya and she reached out to me. It is something Maya does so consistently. Reaching out to people, embracing us. There I was, trying to figure out what it meant to be an editor-in-chief of a magazine, and she called me one day. Afterwards she said, "You know, I'm just a big fan of yours," and I practically dropped the phone. "You are?" She has an incredible way of affirming spirits, and it is the embrace that does it. Maya is an embracer of people, experiences, new experiences, of places, ideas. Arms.

— MARCIA GILLESPIE

Maya believed in me before I believed in myself. She recognized me as a person before she ever heard me play the piano. And in recognizing my potential, she helped me become who I am. It was not long before she adopted me as family and said I could call her auntie, as is the tradition in Ghana among family and friends. She has encouraged me to share my art more willingly and to make it a part of me, rather than have it as a separate interest. Now I teach music. I learned from Auntie Maya to believe in my students before they believe in themselves— or are capable of it. So in a way I try to give back what Maya gave me.

— WILLIAM CHAPMAN NYAHO

"Mostly, what I have
learned so far about aging,
despite the creakiness of
one's bones and the
lumpiness of one's once
silken skin, is this: Do it.
By all means, do it."

— MAYA ANGELOU

She has an absolute rapacious desire to know; she really wants to know about everything, all of the wonderful things and all of the horrible things. There is no real barrier between the private and the public of her world—who she is— she is a totally public figure. In that way, in terms of her thinking, her being, her seeing, she is premodern.

— CONNIE SUTTON

If one were to triangulate the truly multifarious entity that is Maya Angelou, three angles would thrust forth: GENEROSITY, CURIOSITY, CREATIVITY. Maya brings all these to all of the venues and foyers of a life that seems truly charmed, although she has known tragedy, anguish, and disappointment. GENEROSITY is truly her hallmark: it marks her deportment, her relations with friends, family, colleagues, with total strangers, her contacts with institutions and causes, her encounters with all the complications arising from her dynamism and success. Maya's CURIOSITY is deep, serious, perpetual, and above all intellectual, never descending into the merely trivial, always soaring toward the transcendental. Maya wants to know the when, the how, the why; hers is the unending quest of the eternal student, the perennial teacher. CREATIVITY is the essence of Maya Angelou. Here her generosity and curiosity join, intertwine, fuse into constantly evolving constellations of sound, word, sentence, poem, song, essay, encomium, but her creativity is never absent from the morning greeting, always an aubade, from the formal salutation, a triumph of elocution, from the evening valedictory, a benison. Her friends are blessed in such a paragon, as she finds herself blessed in them.

— RICHARD LONG

To sharpen a person's ethos with basic and elementary knowledge is to train the individual mind. One is only educated when one has learned to trace and to cherish self-control, humor, moderation, courage, generosity, and nobleness. These and individual privacy are the true characteristics of democracy—and Maya Angelou.

— MÁRIA TSIAPERA

You're never going to know every-body and you're never going to be able to read all of the books. So when you have a living person who imparts all of that, she can then give you the way it felt, the way it smelled, the way it tasted. An artist like Maya Angelou can make you experience all of those senses and all of that emotion.

— GEORGE FAISON

Maya is a master teacher, always sharing information and knowledge. If you don't grow, you're telling the same stories all the time, but Maya is also a learner— growing, always thinking and never static, which is the mark of a good teacher. She strives for excellence and breadth more than anybody I've ever met.

— RUTH B. LOVE

Oh, I love driving Dr. Angelou around! I get
to meet her family and friends from around the
world. I get to see how she influences people's
lives—how people grow in her presence.
Through my work and being around her, I
have learned a lot more courage and how to be
a better person. Dr. Angelou teaches one to
love and respect one another, to treat others
how you would like to be treated. Her secret is
to read and learn as much as you can.

— JOHN MILES

"I have written of the Black experiences, which I know intimately. I am always talking about the human condition in general and the human being in particular. What it is like to be human, what makes us weep, what makes us fall and stumble and somehow rise and go on from dirtiness into darkness . . ."

— MAYA ANGELOU

Maya doesn't remain down, even living through very different situations and circumstances. You know that she is always going to get up and pursue or persist. And I don't mean just survive—she flourishes, and I think it's because inside she holds positive thoughts and she does a lot of good.

— RUTH B. LOVE

Maya has the kind of passion that is unrelenting. Once her passion is focused on a point, she will press on relentlessly—all the way through. She will put her whole body and soul into her passion with a vigilance and a determination that will not accept anything else other than what she is focused on. She tries as best she can to mingle passion and compassion, to temper it with enough sweetness so that there is strength as well as tenderness; not too much strength to appear a bully and not too much sweetness to appear weak—bittersweetness of compassion and mercy with determination.

— DEFOY GLENN

You don't see aging as long as you stay in the flow of life. One thing Maya says often is: "Life is for the living—as long as you are deep in it, live it fully." Age will only become a factor if one starts to fold up in a shawl and think of oneself. She says to life: "I'm with you, if you are going this way I am too." If things change, get in the group and move with the new. Don't say, "We used to do this, now they are doing that. Say, rather, I am still alive and this is what is being done now, this is what I'm doing—staying with the flow of life; if the stream is going north to south, go north to south." She believes in living life, and although the psychological changes will take place, whatever one does or does not do, the spirit is eternal, and when it is alive and vibrant and in the flow of life, it somehow miraculously retards the aging process. Feeling old has a lot to do with what people expect one is supposed to do, feel, and think at a certain age. If one buys into that, then psychologically one starts to age, thus aiding the physical. But if one does not see or believe in any of that, then one is going to stay vibrant, feel alive. The vibrancy of one's behavior affects how one looks and how one is perceived by people.

— DEFOY GLENN

Maya invariably brings up the positive
side in all negative situations.
Never dwell on the negative, ever, is her message.
"Get up, go on, move on, go for it, work at it."

— VELMA GIBSON WATTS

Many people whose parents
are mountains feel overshadowed,
hemmed in. I feel liberated. She
has shown me what is possible
with perseverance. I too can
construct my own mountain,
and I can start building
on top of hers.

— GUY JOHNSON

Maya has come to believe that
troubles are a blessing.
They force you to change, to believe.
When Jean, my wife, died, Maya
adopted me. She turned up at most
of my political campaigns.
She was always available and always
willing to help, on both a professional
and personal level. She has a saying—
"This is life and you can meet it."

— ANDREW YOUNG

"We need art to live fully and to grow healthily. Without art, we are dry husks drifting aimlessly on every ill wind; our fortunes are without promise and our present without grace."

— MAYA ANGELOU

I guess a lot of writers may have this gift, but when she is performing, she may forget a line or two, but she'll create a new line, something that she's never said before.

— VALERIE SIMPSON

When I'm on stage with Dr. Angelou,
I have a tendency to forget that I'm one of
the performers too, because when she starts
to emote and radiate all over the place, it
affects me. I become one of the people
who came to see her as opposed to one of the
people performing with her. Often I forget
my lines when I'm coming in because I'm so
involved with what she's doing.

— NICK ASHFORD

Who wrote the rule that because one writes a book one shouldn't act, or because one acts one shouldn't dance, or because one dances one shouldn't be a race car driver! The human spirit contains so many hopes and dreams, and to fulfill one's life one should have a chance at doing all these things that call to one's fancy. It might mean taking chances, but why not try! One cannot fail. Maya feels that by the nature of the human brain, we are multifaceted. It is only societal dictate that says some people write, some dance, some sing. WHO WROTE THE RULES? WHY NOT? WHY SHOULDN'T ONE TRY? The human brain is capable of more things than we can imagine, and if one dreams it— and believes it—one certainly should try it. As Maya says, "The human mind is a vast storehouse, there is no limit to it."

— DEFOY GLENN

Her voice is so deep and rich. Watching her on TV was one of the first times I realized how commanding her voice was. You could have your head turned away from the screen and all she would do is speak and you'd turn immediately because her voice carries a sort of culture with it, it says one thing but you hear everything else. I read how in order to make an entrance into a room you have to have two things—to walk well and to speak well. Maya moves gracefully, and her voice embodies so much passion . . . *that's* an entrance.

— NICK ASHFORD

Maya once said to me that it would be easy as an artist to be insane, to play insane, but she said, "You must let them know that you are more normal than anybody, you have to play at being normal." It is hard to do that when you are a creative person, but that is the charge. Maya is a creative person who is able to function in any arena and nobody fears her — that's unusual for a creative person to be able to embrace.

— PHOEBE BEASLEY

Maya belongs to that era of priest-

esses, of chanteuses, of that world

when a dancer, a real creative artist

like an Isadora Duncan, like an Irene

Dunne, like a Pearl Freeman, can

make ritual the highest form of

theater, grabbing our attention and

keeping us riveted to those move-

ments. They're classic. They're

primal. They are the beginning. Just as you think that you've caught up with all that Maya Angelou is doing, she comes forward with a whole new development. She shows another whole realm of creativity, she brings forth a new dimension, moves into another realm.

— GEORGE FAISON

"We must replace fear and chauvinism, hate timidity and apathy, which flow in our national spinal column, with courage, sensitivity, perseverance and, I even dare say, "love." And by "love" I mean that condition in the human spirit so profound it encourages us to develop courage. It is said that courage is the most important of all virtues, because without courage you can't practice any other virtue consistently."

– MAYA ANGELOU

Maya speaks with courage all the time. She talks about courage as a virtue. In most of her presentations she uses this. She has the courage to say, "We are more alike than we are unalike."

— VELMA GIBSON WATTS

Maya is my rock.
Her presence and her spirit sustain me.
More than anything else I have learned from her,
I have learned courage.
Without courage you cannot love, believe, forgive,
be charitable, or have hopes, any of the Bible's virtues.

— CAMPBELL CAWOOD

The two definitive memoirs written in this century are *The Diary of Anne Frank* and *I Know Why the Caged Bird Sings.* In *I Know Why the Caged Bird Sings* Maya did more to break the veil of silence about sexual abuse than anybody I know. At the time she wrote that, nobody was talking about it. She changed the conversation. She brought it out from whispers and she said it way out loud and made it easier for other people to talk who had been gagged. The way in which millions and millions and millions of people all around the world relate to that book speaks to the nerve she struck, a chord. But it was also just the breaking of the silence. A lot of other people have found eloquence.

— MARCIA GILLESPIE

What she did for me personally was to take away the fear of what the next twenty years would be like. Most people as they get older size down. Things get smaller and you don't do as much. But with Maya, everything just gets bigger and grows. I never before focused on the idea that women in their sixties or seventies could be sexy, but through Maya I can see that yes, you can be, you should be, and she is.

— VALERIE SIMPSON

Folks have a right to live and breathe no matter what color, no matter who or what they are. Now they've got cute words for diversity, pluralism and all that, but with Maya these are fundamental and basic beliefs that should be honored and celebrated at all costs. This is one of the things about Maya that really makes her who she is in terms of who her friends are, what she is, what she stands up for, what she believes in, and why she does what she does. That is her driving force. Some people don't feel they have that fundamental right because they may not understand that they have a right as a human being to live, eat, to breathe. One should not tolerate racism or bigotry or prejudice at any cost. One might not be able to respect somebody because they are different but one should not be aggressive or fight them because of it. When one sees Maya with her friends, this is something she lives out. We're not just talking about being rich or poor, famous or unknown, gay or straight. We're talking about a rich tapestry. We're looking at people who may be physically challenged. We're looking at Maya. She mirrors in her life's work, in her actions, that sense of diversity that everyone talks about, but she actually lives it, she breathes it, she walks it.

— BENI IVEY

Maya has helped me to understand courage. As she says, without courage one cannot live out or fulfill the other virtues. So many times it is daring to put the best that you have into an action, even when you're not sure of how it will become but you know that it is something that you have to do. Through all the years that I have known her and followed her, I hear her words because she has made them come alive, not only through language but through her own acts of courage.

— DR. DOROTHY HEIGHT

It's okay to be afraid. It's okay to tell somebody that you're afraid. It's okay to find the courage to go on. Here's the icon of all time, and then she can summon courage in you that she can use and breathe with too.

— GEORGE FAISON

"If you do not appreciate the things you have, other people will treat them with contempt."
– MAYA ANGELOU

Maya often says, "I am a human being and nothing human can be alien to me, and if a human did it, I can do it. I possess the capacity to do it."

— DEFOY GLENN

We have been brought up to think negatively. Our parents only told us when things went wrong. But Maya always says, *"Don't bring the negative to my door."* She projects attention to the positive and helps us know what to work toward. She reminds us to look for the beauty in things.

— ODETTA

Maya wants you to come straight, to be yourself,
no blah, blah, blah. She doesn't believe that women
should take less, and she doesn't believe in putting kid
gloves on because you're a woman.
This is why women take to Maya in such a
very special way, because she can be your sister,
your best girlfriend, your sisterfriend,
your mom and your big sister, all of those things.

— MARCIA GILLESPIE

Be yourself at your best. But also, and
this is so characteristic of Maya,
be aware that most of the world
is made up of others.
You have to see that how or what you
do helps not only yourself but others.
At times you have to take a chance,
a risk to do just that.

— DR. DOROTHY HEIGHT

So strong is the power of her word, so real and so uncompromising in her definition of who she truly is—the spirit, the power, the courage of her soul. She came forth and grabbed me by the shoulders and shook me and said, "Shed the false stuff of who you are, trying to be so white and so proper and so European. . . . so European thinking. Go back to who you are, find out who you are, and tell the truth of who you are."

— JANICE MIRIKITANI

"We need to remember and to teach our children that solitude can be a much-to-be-desired condition. Not only is it acceptable to be alone; at times it is positively to be wished for . . . In the silence we listen to ourselves. Then we ask questions of ourselves. We describe ourselves to ourselves, and in the quietude we may even hear the voice of God."

— MAYA ANGELOU

And she said, "God loves me," until her whole body vibrated with that knowledge. And Maya is that spiritual. And she's also not afraid to voice her spirituality. It's not a question of religion; it's a question of going beyond religion and being able to see the spirituality, the unity in everyone, which is what Maya has done. Not everybody can do it, but Maya can.

— LOUISE MERIWETHER

Does anyone really know what life is all about?

Maya's view is grounded in Christianity, in Christian beliefs. The universe is too complex for there not to be

an overall natural power that is brilliant, that governs, controls, that moves—whatever it does, whatever it is.

I've never bothered to find out what it is—or feel that I have to belong to some sect or religious group. Maya

is a devout Christian, whose belief in the power of prayer is paramount. This is where almost everything that

she does or thinks and believes emanates from—this Christian power, which she utilizes to the fullest. What

I don't think she has confronted is her responsibility in conserving herself in order to be able to do this.

Whatever she perceives as life and its gift comes from a Christian religious base. She was raised in the church,

and her grandmother Henderson was the greatest influence in her life—the mentor, the idol, the icon who

believed in the Lord Jesus Christ and the power of prayer, and that's where Maya takes it from. Maya is a

strong believer in using your gifts—don't squander them, and thank God for your blessings. She always says

these words: "Lord, if you want it said, put it in my mouth."

— M. J. HEWITT

Maya is life—but much bigger than life. It is not just her extraordinary physical presence, it is also the spiritual impact she has on any situation into which she comes. She is somebody who ignites a gathering of people, whether it be a few around a kitchen table or 5,000 at a south London theater.

— JON SNOW

Maya is so true to her vision that she has been assigned by God, or whatever name you may have for that unseen power, to work through the universe. Everything we see in her works with life is God. She is so true to her mission that it is almost overwhelming. She is gracious, but most of all her spirituality is intact. You never have to ask Maya: "Are you a Christian? Are you a Buddhist? Are you a Christian Scientist? or Are you a Baptist?" because her spirituality prevails and one doesn't think about denomination. We all have a line to the power, but you really see it at work in Maya. She can speak to anyone. You feel the spirit of Maya. I don't believe in a God that is somewhere . . . but I believe that God is a presence that resides in us so its creation can be fulfilled through us. When people see Maya or see others who are committed to a mission, they're seeing God at God's best. That's how you know who or what God is. Not just worshipping some deity or somebody that's up in the sky, but a real force, a real presence.

— REV. BARBARA L. KING

When I think of Dr. Maya Angelou, a dear Sister-Friend, I think of her as embodying the values of family and the spirit of the "beloved community," which was the essence of Dr. Martin Luther King Jr.'s dream. A phenomenal woman! She embraces us with her great love, informs us with her profound wisdom, and inspires us with her poetic and artistic genius. A person of uncommon dignity, rare courage, undaunted faith, dogged determination, grace, integrity, and finally, matchless generosity— Maya Angelou is an international treasure.

— CORETTA SCOTT KING

"Love is that condition in the human spirit so profound that it allows one to survive, and better than that, to thrive with passion, compassion and style."
— MAYA ANGELOU

If you want to see a miracle in the twentieth century look at Maya Angelou. The spirit is always moving. It moves to far ends of the earth. A spirit of love, of care, of liberation. Love humanity: that changes the dynamics of evil. Evil cannot stand love. It has to go. And love takes over. Love is liberation. Love liberates. Maya Angelou's spirit liberates.

— REV. CECIL WILLIAMS

You know, some writers live and write in isolation.
Maya may go off to a hotel, or to some little room and write,
but her connection with the world does not stop. She's always
writing from that perspective. The self in relationship to others.
The self in relationship to self. Also, in relationship to other
people and other views, other philosophies, other ways of seeing.
So everyone who reads her work feels as though he or she
knows her; that they've met this person before. I think this is
why her work has such popularity all over the world. There
is something about humanity at large that Maya reflects
in her vision of the world and of others.

— DOLLY A. McPHERSON

She knows what we were born
to discover. Every moment is
important to her, and she brings to each
her love and laughter, and passion for
beauty, for life. She creates a world of
caring around her and sees that it is
good; each smile, each touch,
each kindness offered,
mirroring the grace of God.
That's our beloved Maya.

— SUSAN TAYLOR

I was raised as an only child, but because of my mother I have many brothers and sisters. I share her easily because one cannot own the dew, the snow, the wind, the rain. It is a force of nature. It took no talent to be her son, and I don't see her success as mine. However, her accomplishments lead like stairs to the top of a mountain, and I feel free to climb them.

— GUY JOHNSON

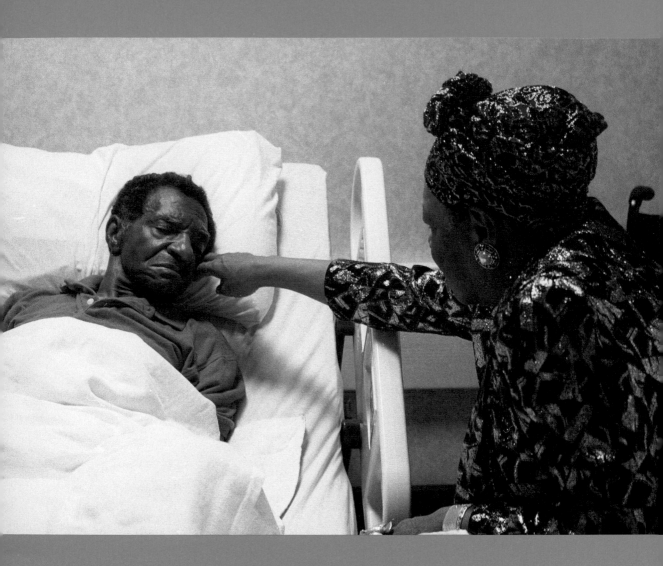

Through Maya I learned the universal gift of healing—who is healing whom. God has blessed each person with the power to heal no matter how grievous the condition as long as each of us has the courage to love unconditionally. You don't have to go to medical school to put balm on an injury or to assuage any pain.

— DR. EDWARD HAPONIK

I call her "Doc," sometimes Mother. She has made me understand that regardless of what life throws at you, if you're strong and confident, you can overcome those problems. I've been with Doc for six years. She has shown me how to take something as simple as a chicken and turn it into a gourmet meal, to use spices and herbs and sauces to make meals more interesting and exciting. I have learned to have confidence in myself. To love and respect myself first.

— MARY THOMAS (MRS. T.)

"I believe the most important single thing, beyond discipline and creativity, in any artistic work, is daring to dare."

– MAYA ANGELOU

She is the embodiment of all the spirits, of all those dancing feelings. Feet and arms and hips and breasts that pulsate to music. Because there is something very, very basic, very earthy about her movements. They liberate us.

— GEORGE FAISON

She's really into movement and dance. And when we're performing, she doesn't stop even though she's not speaking. She's still moving and grooving and getting with the music, and people are just astonished because they think of her as having a different, more stately, quiet manner. Some people wouldn't show that side of themselves to the public, but she's not afraid to let everybody see the many sides of Maya.

— VALERIE SIMPSON

"Risk all, all the time, because we don't know how much time we have to do anything!" One risks every day, everything one does. If it's something one wants to do, then dare to try. Have enough courage to try. It always comes back to courage. Risk all because there is no safety net. Every time one walks out the door, who is to say that one will get back in (or that one goes to the corner store and has a heart attack). Maya also believes that one should not hold onto anything too dear no matter what one has accumulated, because one phone call can inform one that it is all gone, or that all has been burnt in a fire (or that the Stock Exchange has collapsed or there's been a government coup). Possessions, especially material things, all pass in time. The process of decay starts the moment things are created. So, to hold on too tightly prevents one from getting things, because one's hands are so full one cannot take on anything else.

— DEFOY GLENN

MY THANKS AND APPRECIATION GO TO ALL THOSE PEOPLE WHO HAVE GRACIOUSLY
GIVEN THEIR TIME AND THEIR THOUGHTS ON HOW MAYA ANGELOU HAS INFLUENCED OR
TOUCHED THEIR LIVES. MY ONLY REGRET IS NOT BEING ABLE TO STRETCH THE PAGES OF
THIS BOOK TO HOLD THE VOICES OF EACH AND EVERY MEMBER OF MAYA'S EXTENDED FAMILY.
I OWE ENORMOUS GRATITUDE TO ERIC BAKER FOR HIS UNRELENTING
PATIENCE AND PROFESSIONAL EXPERTISE ON THE DESIGN.

I AM GRATEFULLY INDEBTED TO DOLLY McPHERSON AND DEFOY GLENN, TO THE CAPORALES,
TO MY AGENT DAVID CHALFANT, AND ALL THOSE I HAVE WORKED WITH AT
CLARKSON POTTER, ESPECIALLY MY LONG-TIME FRIEND AND EDITOR,
LAUREN SHAKELY, FOR HER CONSTANT REASSURANCE AND SUPPORT.

MY GREATEST DEBT IS TO JUDITH HARRIS FOR HER INTUITION, FOR NURTURING MY
CREATIVE SPIRIT AT A TIME WHEN I NEEDED MOST TO FOCUS ON VALUABLE FRIENDSHIPS
AND PHOTOGRAPHY——A CAUSE THAT GAVE BIRTH TO THIS BOOK.

M.C.C.

Contributors

NICK ASHFORD AND VALERIE SIMPSON
Songwriters and performers,
New York, NY

PHOEBE BEASLEY
Artist and lecturer,
Woodland Hills, CA

CAMPBELL CAWOOD
Investment Manager,
Winston Salem, NC,
and Key West, FL

GEORGE FAISON
Choreographer and President
of Fais-One Productions, Inc.,
New York, NY

MARCIA GILLESPIE
Editor of *Ms.* magazine,
New York, NY

DEFOY GLENN
Actor, Producer, Road
Manager/Assistant and
protégé of Dr. Angelou,
Charlotte, NC

LENNIE GOODINGS
Publisher, Virago Press,
London, England

DR. EDWARD F. HAPONIK
Professor and Clinical
Director, Section on
Pulmonary/Critical Care
Medicine at Wake Forest
University, Wake Forest, NC

DR. DOROTHY HEIGHT
Former President of the
National Council of Negro
Women, Washington, DC

M. J. HEWITT
Fine art consultant, art
curator, and dearest friend
of Maya Angelou,
Santa Monica, CA

BENI IVEY
Executive Director of the
Center for Democratic
Renewal,
Atlanta, GA

GUY JOHNSON
Writer and son,
Oakland, CA

JANICE JONES
Attorney, Montclair, NJ

REV. BARBARA L. KING
Founder and Minister of the
Hillside Chapel & Truth
Center, Writer, Atlanta, GA

CORETTA SCOTT KING
Social activist, Atlanta, GA

CAROLE LEAHY
Music Publisher, London,
England

RICHARD LONG
Professor of Liberal Arts,
Emory University,
Atlanta, GA

RUTH B. LOVE
President of R.B.L.
Enterprises, Professor at San
Francisco State University,
San Francisco, CA

DOLLY A. McPHERSON
Professor of English Studies,
Wake Forest University,
Wake Forest, NC

LOUISE MERIWETHER
Author and Professor,
New York, NY

JOHN MILES
Maya Angelou's assistant and
driver, Winston-Salem, NC

JANICE MIRIKITANI
Poet and President of the
Glide Foundation, Glide
Church, San Francisco, CA

WILLIAM CHAPMAN NYAHO
Professor of Piano, University
of Southwestern Louisiana,
Lafayette, LA

ODETTA (GORDON)
Folksinger, Performer, Civil
Rights Activist, New York, NY

AMELIA PARKER
Former Director,
Congressional Black Caucus,
Currently Consultant for the
Commission on Presidential
Debates, Washington, DC

JON SNOW
TV Anchorman, Channel
Four News, UK

CONNIE SUTTON
Professor of Anthropology,
New York University, NY

MARY THOMAS (MRS. T.)
Dr. Angelou's Housekeeper,
Winston-Salem, NC

SUSAN TAYLOR
Editor-in-Chief, *Essence*
magazine, New York, NY

ELEANOR TRAYLOR
Professor of English, Howard
University, Washington, DC

MÁRIA TSIAPERA
Professor of Linguistics,
University of North Carolina
at Chapel Hill, NC

VELMA GIBSON WATTS
Assistant Dean of Student
Affairs and Director of the
Office of Minority Affairs at
Wake Forest University,
Wake Forest, NC

REV. CECIL WILLIAMS
Minister of Liberation, Glide
Memorial United Methodist
Church, San Francisco, CA

ALICE WINDOM
Social Worker,
St. Louis, MO

THE HONORABLE ANDREW
YOUNG
Co-Chairman of the Good
Works International, LLC;
Past U.S. Ambassador to the
U.N., Atlanta, GA